For B, I love you - H

For Dakota. Love, Mom

Copyright © 2019 by Hadley Barrows

All Rights Reserved. No part of this book may be reproduced in any form without written permission from the publisher.

ISBN 978-0-9904298-3-8

Book design by Megan Moore.
Typeset in Quicksand, Khaki, and SleepyFatCat.
The illustrations in this book are watercolor paintings.

& Then Publishing
www.AndThenPublishing.com

Babella's Umbrella

By Hadley Barrows
Illustrated by Megan Moore

& Then Publishing

What was that **bump, bump**?
Was that the sound of rain?

No. That was a buzzy bumblebee, bumping Babella's umbrella.

What was that **bop, bop**?
Was that the sound of rain?

No. That was a bouncing blackbird, bopping Babella's umbrella.

What was that **brush, brush**?
Was that the sound of rain?

No. That was a bashful butterfly, brushing Babella's umbrella.

What was that **bam, bam**?
Was that the sound of rain?

No. That was a busy beaver, bamming Babella's umbrella.

What was that **boom, boom**?
Was that the sound of rain?

No. That was a baby black bear, booming Babella's umbrella.

About the Author

Hadley Barrows (left) has been a professional writer for more than fifteen years. She taught writing to teens and adults in classes through The Loft, Minneapolis Community Education, private tutoring and other workshops. She has a degree in Journalism from Drake University and a Masters of Business Administration from the Carlson School of Management at the University of Minnesota. She lives in Minneapolis with her husband and two sons.

About the Illustrator

Megan Moore (right) grew up in Huntsville, AL. She studied illustration at the Savannah College of Art and Design. In 2002, she moved to Minneapolis and started her career as an artist. She is a member of Studiopolis, a nine-artist studio in the Northrop King Building. She has shown her art widely in regional galleries, shops and art fairs. Megan does freelance illustration and graphic design work in addition to personal and commissioned paintings. She lives in the Longfellow neighborhood of Minneapolis with her husband, son and daughter. See more of Megan's artwork at www.meganmoore.com.

Hadley and Megan's first book, *Antler, A: A Cabin ABC Book*, is available at **www.andthenpublishing.com**.

Babella's hearing aid and the Ling Six Sounds

The Ling Six Sounds, [m], [ah], [oo], [ee], [sh] and [s], are part of almost every word we say. Babella uses a hearing aid to hear all sounds, including these Ling Six Sounds.

Like Babella, children who are deaf or hard of hearing may use hearing aids or cochlear implants to hear. They practice the Ling Six Sounds to develop their hearing and language skills.

Can you find each of the Ling Six Sounds in *Babella's Umbrella*?

CPSIA information can be obtained
at www.ICGtesting.com
Printed in the USA
LVHW011356050719
623204LV00003B/5/P